Meditation

A Straightforward, Step By Step Guide To Conquering Depression And Anxiety In Order To Regain Control Of Your Life

(Through Natural Pure Awareness Meditation And You May Explore Your Mind)

Winston Jones

TABLE OF CONTENT

Introduction 1
Meditation Focused On Being Mindful 5
Acquiring Skills In The Art Of Breathing 9
Purifying One's Thoughts 18
Alternative Methods Of Meditation 22
What Exactly Does It Mean To Meditate Creatively? 31
Guide To Meditation For Newcomers 37
Suggestions For Increasing Your Optimism, As Well As Your General Emotional And Spiritual Attitude Towards Life 44
Activities To Improve Children's Listening Skills 48
How Is It That Chakras May Be Healed? 56
Meditation On The Pure Pleasures Of Everyday Life 65
The Site Of Great Prospect 74
Having Attained Silence And Finding Contentment 81
Strategies For Meditating For Those Who Are More Experienced 84

Acquiring Knowledge Of The Chakra System . 93

A Short Meditation Session Of Five Minutes Each Time There Is A Break In The Workplace 104

What Is It And Why Should I Do It? 108

Techniques For Beginners Of Meditation 117

Meditation With A Guided Session To Clear Away Mental Clutter 121

Putting Together The Day 132

Introduction

I would like to express my gratitude and offer my congratulations on your successful download of the book "Meditation: The Power of Meditation, The Path to Mastery."

I take it that no one enjoys enduring pain. We don't want to put ourselves through any kind of desolation and deprivation because we don't want to feel wretched; we don't want to go through negative experiences; we don't want to go from one poor episode of our lives to another; and we don't want to go from one bad episode to another. If this is the case, then why do we gravitate towards things that lead us towards enduring suffering?

Why is it that a greater number of individuals have a tendency to think negatively rather than positively? Why is it that the majority of people don't choose to consume healthier meals over junk foods? Why do individuals not exercise more frequently? Why do individuals choose to squander their time on pointless activities when they need to be concentrating on their work?

It may seem on the surface that all of this occurs because we may not truly love ourselves. However, the actual truth is that this vicious cycle of giving in to harmful behaviours occurs because we fail to live in the present in a way that is welcoming, calm, and nonjudgmental.

Because our minds are always wandering to other topics, we often fail to recognise the passage of time as it occurs because we are preoccupied with other things. This is the reason why we are unable to adequately recognise our ideas, feelings, and emotions and respond to them in an appropriate manner.

If you are depressed, you may give in to the financial temptation of using alcohol to numb the sensation rather than recognising the emotion for what it is and diving deeper into it to find effective ways to deal with it. If you do this, however, you will not be able to properly combat the depression. Instead of meditating on the anger and delving deeper into it to see where it comes from, you may start thinking nasty things about the person who has harmed you when you feel furious. This may be because you feel like you have been mistreated.

If you examine your daily routine, the many activities in which you participate, the multitude of unwelcome feelings that you go through, as well as the fact that you are not particularly happy with your life at the moment, you will come to the conclusion that the reason for this is that you are not conscious of both your own actions and the events that take place around you. The word "meditation" is the golden ticket to a lot better, happier, calmer, and more satisfied existence, and the good news is that you can change everything for the better and live a much better life overall. In this book, you will learn more about how you may accomplish this goal via the practise of meditation.

Meditation Focused On Being Mindful

Meditation may help you slow your racing mind, release unpleasant ideas and sensations, enhance sleep, boost memory, generate awareness, and concentrate on the present now. It can also help with depression, decrease stress levels, and make you feel less anxious. It is especially helpful during times of social stress when individuals feel as if they have no control, such as during a pandemic, political war, or environmental calamity. Because of this, there is widespread anxiety, hysteria, stigma, tension, and hostility towards foreigners.

You should give this exercise a try for five minutes each day, and then gradually expand the amount of time you spend on it as your schedule permits.

To help you concentrate on certain parts of your life that you'd want to modify or better, you may want to jot down a few notes before you start this process. After all, you are able to hone your awareness skills via the practise of this sort of meditation.

You may find that aromatherapy with calming essential oils like lavender or sage is helpful in soothing you. The ideal atmosphere for beginning this meditation may also be created by using gentle music from a spa or lighting that is dim.

How to go about it

1. Identify an appropriate amount of time as well as an inviting and peaceful location.

2. Dress in loose-fitting clothes that is comfortable for you.

3. Allow yourself to unwind while you sit, recline, or assume the lotus position.

4. You have the option of looking down, which will cause your eyes to be half-closed, or you may totally shut your eyes.
5. Take a few long, slow breaths and concentrate on drawing air in via your diaphragm while you do so.
6. Bring your attention to each inhale and exhale. Take a few full breaths in with your nose, and then let them out through your lips.
7. Pay attention to the sights, sounds, and smells that are all around you at all times. Additionally, bring your awareness to the feelings that are occurring throughout your body.
8. Let go of any and all distracting ideas, sensations, and other mental constructs.
9. Don't worry if your thoughts keep wandering; that's normal. Bring your attention back slowly to the way you are breathing. Because of this, the practise of mindfulness consists of bringing one's

attention back and forth between the past, the present, and the future.

10. When you are finished, softly open your eyes or elevate your gaze lightly to signal that you are finished.

11. Start with moving your fingers gently, then move the rest of your body, and finish by stretching and saying "thank you." Take a little minute to become aware of the sensations in your body, as well as your thoughts and feelings.

When you say "thank you," you are expressing gratitude to yourself for continuing to meditate, to the higher power that is significant to you for granting you the gift of being able to meditate, to our ancestors for paving the way and enlightening us with the collected wisdom that they have, and to the writers and the internet for spreading the word about this practise.

Acquiring Skills In The Art Of Breathing

If you read the above quote, you'll see that it's really perceptive. What it is telling you is that the extent of the agony you are experiencing is par for the course. It's a perfectly natural response to the stimulus. Therefore, when you experience all of the negative emotions that you do, it is the beginning of the healing process and the beginning of better understanding your life. The way you breathe may also help you have a better knowledge of why you feel such bad things and what those negative emotions and ideas are doing to your body and mind. This can be accomplished by increasing the amount of oxygen that flows into your bloodstream. Beginning the process of gaining a knowledge of the importance of your breathing is an important first step since it is the path that leads to good meditation.

Because one cannot just begin meditating and expect it to be effective, I felt it necessary to organise the information in this book according to a predetermined sequence. Your life has far too many things that might divert your attention, and you also need to learn how to properly detach yourself from the world around you and breathe properly. My instructor and I would often have a good chuckle about this topic since, up to that point in my life, I had never even considered the possibility that breathing was something that required deliberate effort. After all, I had survived each and every year of my existence, which led me to believe that I had some knowledge about the process of respiration. I could not have been more off in my assumptions. Anxious individuals are sometimes provided with a paper bag to breathe into as a means of easing their concerns. This is not some outdated urban legend. It does assist due to the fact that when you are worried, you have a tendency to overoxygenate, which means that you breathe more quickly and allow too much air to get into your body, pushing it into stress mode. When you do this, it sends your body into stress mode. Your stress level and blood pressure both increase, and your blood pressure continues to climb.

You may not realise it, but if you have a negative attitude, you tend to repeat the same behaviour. What do you believe are the physical manifestations of anger? You may reply to anything with an angry response; but, if you let the anger to build up, you will not breathe properly, and the increased amount of oxygen in your body will force you to react in a highly unreasonable manner because of what the increased oxygen is doing to your body. Imagine that your body is a piece of machinery. If you give it an excessive amount of fuel, it will function too rapidly, but that does not necessarily indicate that it is operating efficiently. It's possible that you won't feel like you're getting enough oxygen. You could get the impression that you are unable to breathe normally, but the truth is that the paper bag that is being passed around for people to breathe in and out of is helping to bring the oxygen levels back up to normal so that the feeling of fear is gone. When you hyperventilate, what ends up happening is that every blood ventricle in your body goes into overdrive and begins to respond. At that point, a feeling of helplessness and fear will come over you.

People are more likely to breathe through their mouths rather than their nostrils, and this trend is expected to continue. Observe a smoker and you'll see that they tend to take their breaths via their mouths more often than not. Some individuals, even those who do not smoke, have the habit of breathing through their mouths rather than their noses in the incorrect notion that this would allow them to take in a greater volume of air. You will find that it is beneficial to your meditation practise if you regularly engage in deep breathing.

Practise taking long, slow breaths.
For this exercise, you are going to lay down on the bed, but instead of using two pillows, you are just going to use one. This is due to the fact that when your head is held higher, your windpipe becomes less open, which makes it more difficult to breathe. If you watch medical

dramas on television, you've probably seen how the emergency room personnel tilts a patient's head back so that they may place a tube to assist the patient in breathing. It is much simpler to enter that tube into the head when it is tilted at the appropriate angle, just as it is simpler for you to breathe if you tilt your head slightly backward.

First, inhale through the nose for the count of eight, then hold your breath for the same amount of time, and finally, exhale through the nose for the count of ten.

Feel the air in the upper portion of the diaphragm as you continue to breathe in and out in this manner. Also, notice how the diaphragm nearly rocks back and forth as you exhale. This is what I want you to focus on as you continue to breathe in and out in this manner. Keep your hand there and concentrate on being aware of it. You should make this a regular part of your routine for at least a few days before you ever start to meditate. The reason for this is that this method of breathing needs to become automatic, and it also needs to be something that feels natural, so that when you meditate, you do not experience discomfort as a result of having to change the way that you breathe and having to concentrate on that more than meditation requires you to concentrate on the act of meditation itself.

Now give this a go. Keep your thumb over your left nostril as you breathe normally. Inhale via the right nostril and exhale through the left. Maintain the same hold on your breath that you did previously, but this time move your thumb to the opposite nostril. Take a breath out of the nostril that is not blocked. You should do this exercise while sitting upright, and you should aim to complete it around nine times. This particular kind of breathing is known as NadiShodhan Pranayama, and it is highly recommended to do before to beginning a session of meditation. It helps to prepare your mind for meditation while also bringing your attention to the "now" in the present moment. It is also an excellent exercise for balancing out the various regions of the brain that are responsible for different types of reasoning, such as logical thinking and emotional thinking. The purpose of this is to facilitate the natural flow of "prana" throughout your body. Because "prana" is the Sanskrit word for "life force," using this kind of breathing exercise can help you feel better, make you more alert and balanced, and improve your ability to focus. The feeling that you are pushing your breath is the single most crucial thing to avoid while practising this sort of breathing; you should never give yourself that impression. It need to have a calm and easy feel about it. Holding your thumb over one nostril while forcing the other to do all the work is not a natural thing to do, but if you take it gently and are kind with yourself, you will realise the advantages of doing so.

Purifying One's Thoughts

In addition to meditating, there are a few other things you can do that will help clear your mind, which, in turn, will make the atmosphere around you more conducive to adopting a Zen mentality. It is very improbable that an individual who has a clean workstation and uncluttered bedroom would also have an uncluttered mind. It is quite improbable that you are in Zen mode if you do not have the time to tidy your room, take a shower, make yourself seem presentable, and have time to yourself. De-cluttering your life may be accomplished via the practise of a variety of different Zen habits. Although the list might go on forever, here are a few examples to get you started:

Every morning, you should make your bed.

Organise the icons on your computer's desktop such that there are less than ten of them. Keep just a few tabs open at any one time.

Immediately after each meal, wash the dishes in the washbasin.

Clear off your workstation.

Take care of one task at a time.

Get rid of the additional things you're doing that are just wasting your time.

Try going a whole week without using any kind of technology or media.

Consume food slowly and with awareness.

Turn off all of your electronic devices and try to go to bed at a decent hour.

Arrive to the office 10 minutes early.

Make sure you give yourself some additional time to unwind each morning before you go to work.

Before going to bed or when you wake up, write down three things for which you are thankful.

Put in writing three tasks that need to be finished each day, and come to an agreement that you won't concentrate on or worry about anything else.

If it's at all feasible, try listening to binaural beats or solfeggio frequencies while you're at work or on the way there.

Only read stuff that is of a good quality and is encouraging rather than reading click bait articles online.

These are all very significant points. Because there are things that you can do that will keep you in charge of your own mind, but there are also things that tend to promote being a slave to your own brain. Because of this, although there are things that you can do that will keep you in control of your own mind. Technology and stress in all of its manifestations are the primary culprits in this case. You are probably not in a Zen state if you are attempting to juggle too many different activities at once. People who are in a Zen frame of mind are able to focus entirely on one task at a time, without being sidetracked by any other concerns. In the end, this means that they accomplish everything perfectly. Under the pretext of making life simpler, the plethora of additional programmes and technology available on smartphones almost always make things more difficult. A further beneficial habit is always allowing plenty of time for everything. However, in order for these routines to become a natural part of your lifestyle, you will need to place a strong emphasis on maintaining them on a daily basis.

Alternative Methods Of Meditation

There are many different ways to practise meditation. It is possible for it to be active, particularly when the mind and the body are together. It also might consist of doing nothing more than sitting there and not thinking at all. Both yoga and Tai chi, which originate in India and China respectively, are examples of different civilizations' applications of the notion of movement meditation. Visualisation and deep breathing are two practises that may help bring the mind and the body together. As a consequence of this, the dynamic body-mind systems are beneficial to an individual's overall health.

You are able to meditate when you practise yoga because it brings the mind, body, breath, and spirit into balance. In addition, maintaining focus is essential for every stance.

In Tai chi, the coordination of the mind and body is achieved via the use of movements that are both balanced and relaxing. This practise leads to improvements in both one's health and one's knowledge of oneself.

The mind-body systems provide a person with a multitude of useful advantages. They not only enhance mental alertness and attention but also offer flexibility and suppleness to the body as well.

Not Giving Any Thought to It

You are already familiar with the four (4) crucial stages that are involved in meditation. You may be wondering whether it is even possible to meditate if all you do is sit quietly and try not to think about anything. Yes, very much so!

"Just sitting" is what zazen literally implies. This is one of the most important practises in Zen Buddhism, and it is traditionally carried out with one's back to a wall in order to block off any potential distractions. At this point, you will not be required to visualise any particular topic, visuals, or symbols. The purpose of doing zazen is to simply watch what is going on in your mind without allowing your attention to be drawn away by your own ideas.

It is encouraged that during zazen, you think about absolutely nothing at all. You may also bring your complete consciousness to the act of watching your breath. The goal of this kind of meditation is to assist you attain mental calm by training you to exert control over your thoughts. Imagine a monkey that is always talking. Are you aware of how frustrating it may be when they hop from one branch to another? They never stop moving and never stop moving once they start. Buddhism likens this to a mind that has not been trained. A mind that is crowded just skips from one concept to the next, much like a monkey that is always chattering. Because of this, you find that you have a lot of thoughts, which in turn causes you tension and anxiety.

The good news is that you may learn to silence the chattering monkey inside you by training yourself to be aware of the stream of ideas that are running through your mind. And this is something that may be accomplished by meditating.

Is it true that being sedentary is a waste of time? It is a fallacy to believe that sitting still and doing nothing at all is only a waste of valuable time. If you are used to leading a hectic lifestyle, sitting still and doing nothing at all may seem uncomfortable at first. You may train your mind to be more productive by sitting motionless for long periods of time. After an emotionally taxing experience, such as an exam at school or a presentation at work, it is similar to giving your mind a chance to recharge. Recharging one's mind and body with even just a few minutes of alone each day is beneficial. This is not at all a productive use of one's time. Instead, you are efficiently using the time that you have available.

The vast majority of individuals are guilty of this, yet they are really doing themselves a tremendous favour by doing so. Therefore, make it a habit to sit motionless and give yourself some time to yourself every day. The advantages are incredible, to say the least.

Find some space in your mind.

If you often get the impression that your brain is crowded with a great number of unpleasant ideas, it is possible that the moment has come for you to create some mental space. Learn to halt whenever you become aware that there is just a little gap between the conclusion of one idea and the beginning of the next one. This lull in activity, however brief it may be, has the potential to significantly improve the quality of your life. It is similar to making an effort to relax one's thoughts, and with practise, you will find that you have less of a cluttered head.

Your current state of consciousness

Consider the contents of your mind, including your ideas and everything else that pops into your head, to be a stream of consciousness. To begin meditating and bringing peace to your mind, just sit quietly and observe how each idea enters and leaves your head. Give it a go for a few minutes and pay attention to how it affects you during that time. You could feel self-conscious when you first start the meditation session, but after a while, everything will start to seem more typical and natural to you. When you meditate in this manner, you will find that in a very short period of time, long-forgotten memories will come flooding back to you, and ideas for the future will begin to take shape. You could even stumble onto forgotten memories that you were completely unaware of in the past.

Observe that when your mind is untrained, everything seems to be a jumble of confused elements; these are ideas and connections that are lingering in your mind that are not linked to one another and are unusual. If, on the other hand, you have a mind that has been taught, the flow of ideas will be organised, producing order inside your mind. When you have mastered this skill, you will no longer be in the same position as the babbling monkey that was discussed previously.

Having attained Silence and Finding Contentment

Because of the hectic lifestyles that most people lead, the background noise that they experience on a daily basis has likely become something that they can tolerate. But were you aware that one's life may still have moments of stillness even when it is filled with chaos? Keep in mind that allowing certain periods of stillness into your life might bring about a sense of calm when you do so. This is something you can put into practise in your regular life.

To provide just a few instances, you might try shutting off the radio or the television and simply sitting there in quiet for a few minutes. When there is chaos at home, you have the option of consciously choose quiet by deciding not to contribute more to an already heated quarrel. You will benefit from this practise in situations in which it is difficult or impossible to avoid noise. Therefore, you should step away from the cacophony and pay closer attention to the myriad noises that are occurring around you. When you begin to meditate, you will gradually develop a greater appreciation for what it is like to experience life to the fullest, free from the pressures and ambiguity that often accompany such an endeavour.

At Long Last Discovering Peace

Relax your body and mind completely by settling into a comfortable position. Focus your attention on your breath as you enter your own personal meditative state. When distractions appear, you should just let them flow through your thoughts and then return your focus to where it was before. Stay seated with a calm state of mind and concentrate on observing your breath. Make the most of the natural space you have, and focus on being present in the now. When you make this a consistent part of your life, you will come to understand that you can find inner calm even in the most hectic and harried environments. Keep in mind that the more you do this, the more the quality of your life will improve as a result of your efforts.

What Exactly Does It Mean To Meditate Creatively?

When we go back in time to the period of our ancestors, we find that they devised a method of relaxing that is now known as meditation. It is possible to trace its beginnings and origins all the way back to prehistoric times. So, what exactly does it mean to meditate? To "think deeply and focus one's mind for a period of time, in silence or with the aid of chanting, for religious or spiritual purposes or as a method of relaxation," this is how the dictionary defines meditation.

When people think about meditation, one of the most common images that comes to mind is Buddha. Back in the year 500 BC, when his teachings were carried throughout Asia and disseminated to other parts of the continent, he made his first impression on history.

Here we are in the present day, when we are surrounded by a multitude of devices and an abundance of activities. The pace of life is quickening, which results in an increase in levels of stress. Meditation is becoming more popular as a means of relaxation, stress management, and finding serenity in one's life as a response to this growing trend.

There is a wide variety of meditation that has developed through time within a variety of religious and spiritual traditions. Some of these traditions include Buddhism, Christianity, and Hinduism, to mention a few. The following are some of the most prevalent forms of meditation:

The ability to focus one's attention is the primary need for successful meditation. Training oneself in various methods of focus may be considered a sort of meditation in and of itself, and can also serve as a gateway into other types of meditation.

There are many different kinds of meditation practises that may assist you in overcoming distractions and improving your capacity to focus on one thing at a time. You may improve your focus by a variety of practises, some of which include Zen meditation, transcendental meditation, Om meditation, Shine meditation or Samadhi meditation, and chakra meditation, to mention just a few.

• Reflective meditation, often called analytical meditation, is a kind of meditation in which one practises controlled thought. If you want to be effective with this kind of meditation, you are going to need to choose a question, a subject, or a theme, and then sit with it. At initially, there is a good chance that your mind may stray to other subjects; nevertheless, the purpose of the practise is to teach your mind to return to the subject at hand once it has wandered off. This method of meditating on a topic or subject may provide profound insight and answers to the practitioner.

- Mindfulness meditation is one of the major forms of meditation that may help you learn a basic thing, which is to pay attention or to be "mindful." This is one of the things that you can learn through practising mindfulness meditation. It is well known that this particular kind of meditation may bring pain relief as well as assistance for individuals who are suffering from anxiety and sadness. You may practise several methods that fall under this category, such as mindful eating, deep breathing meditation, body scan meditation, visualisation meditation, and walking meditation, as well as sitting meditation and walking meditation.

• Meditation with a Focus on the Heart: This kind of meditation assists in opening the heart chakra and purges the body of any bad energy that may be present. It may help alleviate depression, improve a poor body image, and other areas of one's life in which love and acceptance are lacking. It can also bring more love and pleasure into one's life.

• Creative Meditation is a distinct sort of meditation method since this form of meditation will help you to intentionally nurture as well as enhance a variety of traits of your mind. This style of meditation was named "creative" because it was first developed by artists. This meditation focuses on enhancing traits such as appreciation, joy, compassion, patience, empathy, love, gratitude, humility, fearlessness, and sensitivity, amongst other positive attributes. The practise of creative meditation may be analogous to the practise of being an overall more improved person.

Guide To Meditation For Newcomers

Meditation might first seem overwhelming or impossible to beginners. This is OK. This is quite normal, and things will only get better from here. Meditation is a skill that has to be practised. After all, it is quite the undertaking. It is vital that you continue to practise and perfect the skill of meditation in order to reap the benefits, thus it goes without saying that you should keep on keeping on.

When you are anxious, it might be challenging to focus on a single topic for an extended period of time, which is necessary for the practise of meditation. You are going to want to begin your practise of meditation with concentration meditation since it is the most straightforward of the several kinds of meditation. Finding the concentration necessary for effective meditation may be accomplished by concentrating on a single mantra and your breathing at the same time. You may focus your attention on anything in the immediate environment, such as the wick of a candle or the tip of a pen; the choice is entirely up to you. As soon as you start concentrating on the thing that you have chosen, you will stop paying attention to the other things that are going through your head and instead give your whole attention to the thing that you are concentrating on. Even while it isn't always simple, if you put in the effort to perfect this talent via practise, there is nothing in this world that will make you feel more at ease.

Finding a spot in your house that is both comfortable and spotless is essential for meditation. When individuals meditate, they often sit on the floor and cross their legs; however, if this is not feasible, they may always use a chair or a meditation cushion instead of sitting on the floor. In any case, it is a wise decision to have a meditation cushion within easy reach for whenever you may need it.

When you want to meditate, you need to be sure that you have had enough sleep. In order to get the most out of your session, you need to make sure that your mind is as fresh and awake as it possibly can be. Before beginning your meditation session, check to make sure that you have not taken any form of medicine or ingested any alcohol.

Before beginning to practise meditation, make sure that you have had enough rest and that your stomach is not too full. This is just as vital as making sure that you are well-rested. It is much more difficult to meditate while one's stomach is full, therefore whenever it is feasible, make sure that you have not eaten anything for at least two hours before to your meditation session. If this is not possible, try to avoid meditating on an empty stomach.

You are now prepared to get started! Make sure that you begin by dressing in something that is comfortable. If you can help it, steer clear of jeans. While you are meditating, you should take off your shoes since there is a significant likelihood that you will desire to do so. If you'd rather wear socks, that's also OK.

Reduce the brightness of the lights in the room. If you choose to utilise candles during your meditation, now is the moment to light them up. In addition, you may bring things that make you happy into the space where you meditate, such as flowers, incense, and other such things.

Now, with your back straight, sit down on the floor (or on a chair, if you've decided to use one) and I'll show you where to put your hands. If you are sitting on a chair, propping yourself up using pillows and cushions is a totally acceptable method of doing so. You should now remain motionless in the posture that you have selected and start concentrating on your breathing as soon as you can. When you find that your thoughts have wandered away from the activity at hand, bring your attention back to the act of breathing. You should take calm breaths in and out, and you should keep thinking about those breaths so that you may become aware of how you feel when you inhale and exhale. You may choose to close your eyes if you prefer. Always keep your attention fixed on the breath that you are taking and centre your thoughts on that single inhale and exhale. After a few minutes of sitting in your quiet potion, you should feel as if your mind has disconnected from the outside world and the rest of your thoughts. Keep your attention completely on the act of breathing, concentrating on each individual breath.

You might also concentrate on a single mantra (which could be a word or an item) and repeat it again and over until you are able to focus your attention completely on that phrase or thing. Again, if you find that your mind is wandering and thinking about other things, you should just pause, bring your attention back to your mantra, and then begin meditating once again.

Beginners often find this to be the most challenging aspect of the practise. If you find that you are unable to concentrate as much as you would want to, try not to be too harsh on yourself about it. Conquering this requires a significant amount of practise, and the more practise you put in, the simpler it will become for you as time goes on.

This is a meditation session, and this is how it should be done. It is so simple, but intricate all at the same time. When you have achieved a level of mastery in meditation and can empty your mind completely, you will question why you did not begin practising meditation earlier.

Suggestions For Increasing Your Optimism, As Well As Your General Emotional And Spiritual Attitude Towards Life

When you have a more optimistic perspective on life, you will experience increased levels of happiness and contentment. When you have a more optimistic perspective on life, you become a beam of sunshine to the people who know you, and both your life and the connections you have become usually easier, happier, and more rewarding. The following are some suggestions on how to cultivate a more optimistic, compassionate, emotionally supportive, and spiritual outlook on life:
Follow the "Golden Rule," which states that you should always treat other people the way you would want to be treated yourself. Keep in mind that God dwells deep inside each of us. Whatever

you do to other people, remember that you are also doing it to your Creator since our bodies are the temples in which the Divine resides. Be kind and patient with others. Always keep in mind that the majority of us are waging a struggle, and because of this, be thoughtful to others.

Be present in your life and try not to waste too much time lamenting past mistakes or missed opportunities. Let go of your errors and the things you regret from the past. It is essential to ignore one's worries and just take pleasure in the here and now.

Always have an attitude of gratitude, since this simple gesture is one of the most effective ways to increase the amount of joy in your life. When you count your blessings instead of your problems, you become closer to God and find it much simpler to take a more optimistic attitude on life.

Quit comparing yourself unfavourably to other people – Everyone is engaged in their own unique struggles. Stop making comparisons between your life and the lives of other people; everyone of us has a unique burden to bear. Comparison on a continual basis will only serve to bring about sadness and discontent.

Imagine what you want to happen, rather of focusing on what you do not want to happen as you use visualisation. You'll be able to unwind and enjoy yourself more as a result of this. In addition to this, it has been shown that engaging in this activity may bring you whatever it is in life that you want.

Laugh often — tell jokes frequently, watch comedies on Netflix or YouTube, and think back on humorous times in your life. People who laugh more tend to report higher levels of happiness and a more optimistic outlook.

Maintaining a state of mental tranquilly and being optimistic need to be second nature to you. You will unquestionably have a better life if you make meditation a regular part of your routine and participate in other activities that teach you to appreciate the here and now.

Activities To Improve Children's Listening Skills

Being attentive requires an active participation in listening. Therefore, the most important step in teaching your kid how to be attentive is to show them how to listen in a variety of ways. This is the pinnacle of what they will learn. Your kid must be able to listen to you, to themselves, to their body, and to others in order for them to be attentive. Your kid has to be able to confide in you, talk to you, and understand that you are listening to them in the manner that they need you to. They have to be able to trust you.

However, even with the most cooperative of youngsters, it may be a challenging effort to encourage and educate your kid to listen to what you have to say. In most cases, this is due to the fact that the conventional techniques used to instruct a youngster in such a skill are tedious and fail to maintain the child's attention and interest. Because of this, child psychologists and paediatricians have collaborated to produce a variety of games that may assist in instructing a kid how to listen more attentively. These games can be found here. These games and activities may, in turn, assist to create trust and communication between you and your kid, which is a win-win situation for everyone involved. Your youngster will not be able to learn how to become more attentive and open with themselves without both of these components. Furthermore, engaging in these various activities alongside your kid may help strengthen the respect that exists between the two of you. This is because your child will notice that you are making an effort to comprehend the world through their eyes when you participate in the same activities that they do.

Naturally, they will not tell you in so many words that this is how you are making them feel since they do not want to offend you. Instead, they will inform you by demonstrating how they react to what you ask of them and how they behave when you speak to them (Halloran, 2020). They will do this by demonstrating how they respond to what you ask of them.

Dance in the Freeze

The first game in the series of listening exercises that will help your youngster improve their listening abilities is the frozen dance game. This is an old-school version of the game, in which a sound or piece of music is played in the background while the youngster is free to move and dance whatever they choose. They are to remain perfectly motionless until they once again hear the music playing, even if the sound and the music suddenly cease playing. Your child's listening abilities will improve as a result of this activity since it requires them to identify times when they are hearing the music and times when they are not hearing it. Adjusting the loudness of the game's soundtrack is one way to provide older kids with a somewhat greater challenge than younger players. At first, turn up the volume of the music so that it is easy to hear when there are gaps in the performance. Then, while the game continues, gradually turn down the volume to make it more difficult for your youngster to hear what is going on. You will be giving kids the opportunity to improve their own abilities in attentive listening if you do so.

Join them in their dancing to inspire them to participate more actively in the game. In point of fact, you should sometimes dance when there is no music playing and maintain a still position when there is music playing. Your kid will acquire additional listening and attention skills as a result of this activity, as they will be able to see that you are not playing the game correctly and bring this out to you. In addition, if your kid is old enough, you should let them take control of the music for a few rounds, stopping it when they want to and beginning it when they want to. This will assist to motivate them during the game as well as retain their interest and attention throughout the competition.

The Finish Line for the Word Game

The end of the word game is an additional activity that may assist in the development of your child's listening abilities. For this game, decide on a topic from which you will choose words, then play accordingly. The next step is for each of you to utter a word that starts with the last letter or sound of the word that came before it. In the beginning, you will be required to choose the game approach, which will consist of either determining the word by its last letter or its final sound. For instance, if the topic you choose is animals and you start the game by using the word "giraffe," your kid will then respond with an animal whose name begins with either the letter F or E, depending on the way of play that you select. Therefore, the frog and the elephant are both candidates for this question's response. Although it is common knowledge that the word "giraffe" is pronounced without the last letter "e," this particular example adheres to the rule of the game that employs the final sound of the word. Which variation of the game you engage in will depend on whether or not your kid is of an appropriate age to be taught how to spell the words. It is essential to the success of this game that none of the words on the list—in this example, the names of the animals—are duplicated.

Because they have to pay attention to the word you are saying and come up with a word that starts with the same sound, this game may help your kid improve their listening skills as well as their ability to remember information. In addition to this, students are required to recall the words that have previously been said.

Away, then, on the green light

The game of "Red Light, Green Light" is the fourth kind of listening exercise that you may use to teach your kid to listen better. In the game of Red Light, Green Light, one player starts by standing a considerable distance away from the other. "Green light!" is shouted by the one who is facing away from the other person and is standing. As a direct consequence of this, the other players start to rush and approach the other player. Someone standing a considerable distance away will yell "Red light!" at random intervals. All of the other players are required to cease running and moving at this moment. This procedure is continued until the person screaming believes the players are near enough for them to be able to turn around and tag each other. The person who is tagged first becomes the "shouter" in the game.

Because the kid is required to listen for the instructions—whether it be a red light or a green light—and respond accordingly, this game helps children strengthen their listening abilities. In addition, if the youngster is taking on the role of the "shouter," they have the additional responsibility of paying great attention to their surroundings in order to determine whether or not somebody is near enough to them to tag. Because it combines active play with the development of listening skills, this game often yields positive results.

How Is It That Chakras May Be Healed?

On the next pages, we will talk about the signs that a chakra is blocked or otherwise imbalanced and how to treat them. If you suspect that one or more of your chakras are blocked, know that you are not alone in this diagnosis. The majority of individuals in western societies, and particularly in the contemporary world, lead lifestyles that are unhealthy and imbalanced. When it comes to the state of their chakras, the vast majority of individuals probably have some degree of imbalance. This is a reasonable assumption to make. Sadly, as our society becomes more materialistic and atheistic in its ideas, a large number of individuals are either completely unaware of this or unwilling to even entertain the possibility that they need treatment that goes beyond the physical realm.

Your chakras may be healed, brought into balance, and awakened via the use of a variety of techniques. Meditation on a daily basis is the key technique that is used. We are going to talk about many methods that you may meditate for a little amount of time each day that will have a significant impact on the chakras' ability to heal.

Healing the chakras may also be accomplished by the practise of yoga, the repetition of daily affirmations, and the judicious use of colour. Crystals are also used by a lot of individuals because of the vibrational qualities they possess and the fact that they are able to store and transfer vibrational spiritual energy. The spiritual components or essence that are connected to the meaning of each of the chakras are tied to the vibrational frequencies that are associated with the chakras.

The seven primary chakras will be discussed in the subsequent parts of this article. Each will be examined in more depth, and the book will spend an entire to analysing only that subject.

Bringing harmony to the Chakras

In the s that are to come, we are going to discuss in further depth the signs that indicate a particular chakra is blocked, as well as the particular techniques that may be used to repair and unblock each of the seven primary energy centres in the body. In this section, we will go through the fundamental steps that make up the healing process for your chakras.

There is going to be the desire, especially if you are a newbie, to jump forward and start focusing on the spiritual chakras. If you are new to this way of thinking, however, there is a good possibility that you have at least some degree of blockages happening in your lower chakras. These blockages may manifest in a number of different ways. Before attempting to deal with the higher-level chakras, it is necessary to first repair the lower chakras in order to ensure that the right balance is maintained. Imagine, for instance, that you have something blocking your root chakra and that as a result you are having trouble with the most fundamental aspects of your existence. You are going to be flooded with a great deal of bad energy, which is going to have an effect on as well as obstruct the higher-level chakras in your body. Will you be able to direct your energy towards unconditional love, speaking the truth, and developing your psychic talents if the root chakra in your body is blocked, causing you to constantly feel insecure and anxious? Although it's possible that some individuals may be successful in doing so, the fact is that the great majority of people won't be able to pull this off successfully. Consider this process to be similar to constructing a home. You start by laying the foundation, and if it is not appropriately built, the remainder of the structure will be unstable and hazardous. You are on a spiritual journey that will last your whole life, so have patience while you work towards achieving your objectives. Those who are able to exercise patience will be rewarded more handsomely.

There are seven different approaches to healing and balancing your chakras, which will help you achieve the highest possible level of physical, mental, emotional, and spiritual health. Following is a condensed explanation of each of them.

Meditation Meditation is beneficial on a variety of ways. Meditation is a practise that may help you to clear your thoughts and relax your nerves. You may work with each of the chakras by using various visualisation methods throughout your meditation time. In the next s, we will go through the particulars as well as some fundamental approaches to meditation.

Yoga

Yoga is something that you may choose to practise or not, but if you do decide to, it can be a really helpful tool for you. You may physically open up your chakras with the use of yoga, which will increase the flow of natural energy. In addition to assisting in the healing process and restoring balance to your chakras, it also has numerous positive effects on the body, including increased flexibility and muscle tone.

Taking in Air

Meditation and yoga may be practised in combination with deep breathing techniques, or they can be practised on their own. The nervous system may be soothed and the flow of energy throughout the body can be opened up by practising deep breathing.

Sound production and vocalisation

There are a lot of different methods to connect a sound with the process of healing the chakras. You may, for instance, try using single tones or mantras. You may also try saying daily affirmations to help "reprogram" your subconscious mind and get you closer to achieving your objectives. This will be of great assistance to you. Music is another tool that may be used to help you succeed in your endeavours.

Different hues

There are seven primary chakras, and each one is linked to a certain hue that serves as a representation of its corresponding energy frequency. You may help yourself focus on a particular chakra by surrounding yourself with the colours that are connected with that chakra. This may be accomplished via the use of crystals and garments that you wear, take with you, or employ in your meditation practise. In addition to this, it incorporates the colours that are utilised to decorate the space, as well as a room that may be used for doing yoga or meditation.

Food

It is also essential that you choose the nutritious meals that are necessary for the healing of your chakras. You are free to follow the cues provided by the colours. It is not how people in the West often think about things, yet the intensity of a food item's colour may be used to estimate the amount of energy it contains. If you are focused on repairing the root chakra, for instance, you should increase the amount and variety of foods in your diet that are red in colour. This will help stimulate the root chakra.

The Most Important Oils

Essential oils are yet another tool at your disposal for assisting in the healing of your chakras. Each essential oil is also resonating at its own unique frequency of energy vibration. Essential oils may be absorbed via the skin or by inhalation of their aromas.

In the next , we will begin our exploration of the chakra system with the root chakra. In this article, we will investigate the root chakra in depth and talk about the signs of a blocked root chakra so that readers will be able to assess for themselves whether or not their root chakra is obstructed.

Meditation On The Pure Pleasures Of Everyday Life

Put the outside world behind you and set out on a path to discover the pleasure that is inside you. Find a spot where you may quiet your thoughts, unwind your body, and become one with the calm that resides inside you.

Turn your attention to your breath while you close your eyes.

First, take a deep breath in, then let it out.

First, take a deep breath in, then let it out.

First, take a deep breath in, then let it out.

Imagine that you are on a beach with sand and that the sky is clear and the sun is shining. You look up to see the sun just rising, and a refreshing wind is blowing in your face.

You have a peaceful disposition, a sense of comfort, and contentment with your existence.

You are standing carefree on a beach all to yourself, oblivious to the outside world. You have a plenty of opportunities to spend time alone with your emotions and ideas.

You have a peaceful disposition, a sense of comfort, and contentment with your existence.

The sound of waves lazily crashing into the coast is what you are now listening to. You decide to stroll towards the ocean, and as you do so, you become aware of the sensation of chilly water under your feet.

You have a peaceful disposition, a sense of comfort, and contentment with your existence.

Imagine for a moment that you are standing on a grassy hill in the middle of the day. You are about to see one of the most breathtaking sunsets ever as the sun begins to drop behind the hills.

You have a peaceful disposition, a sense of comfort, and contentment with your existence.

You are standing on the ground close to the woods, and without having any unfavourable thoughts in your head. You have a plenty of opportunities to spend time alone with your emotions and ideas.

You have a peaceful disposition, a sense of comfort, and contentment with your existence.

You are in the countryside, and you can just make out the sound of birds singing. You begin out in the direction of the setting sun, and as you walk, you feel the cool grass under your feet.

You have a peaceful disposition, a sense of comfort, and contentment with your existence.

Now picture yourself on top of a hill, looking out at the star-filled night sky below you. The moon is shining brightly, and you can make out a myriad of twinkling stars in the sky above you.

You have a peaceful disposition, a sense of comfort, and contentment with your existence.

You are completely at ease while being in the most precarious position imaginable. You have a plenty of opportunities to spend time alone with your emotions and ideas.

You are happy and at peace with your life, and this makes you feel pleased.

The sound you are hearing is that of a soft wind rustling the leaves as it passes through the area. You go out into a path that is lighted only by the moon, and the earth under your feet is pleasantly cold.

You have a sense of satisfaction, calm, and ease with the way your life is going.

You have an attitude of gratitude for the mundane but meaningful aspects of your life.

You are free to meditate for as many minutes or hours as you see fit.

When you are ready, slowly open your eyes and greet the new day with a cheerful expression on your face.

The Fifth, Sixth, and Seventh Points of Posture in 4

The next step in achieving good meditation is to concentrate on your chin, jaw, and eyes to ensure that you are maintaining the proper 7-point posture.

The fifth point of posture is to tuck your chin in towards your chest.

Once you've found a comfortable position, give your chin a very tiny tuck while you do so. It is best to avoid pointing upwards since doing so might put unnecessary pressure on the neck. Also, make sure that you are not looking entirely downwards, either at the ground or at your lap, since this might put additional strain on your neck and lead you to get exhausted more quickly. The act of subtly tucking the chin in towards the chest conveys a sense of humility and assists in maintaining a grounded state, which is one of the primary goals of meditation.

The sixth point of posture is to have an open jaw.

Maintain the position of your tongue on the roof of your mouth to facilitate easy breathing, and then slowly and gently relax the muscles in your face to slightly open your jaw. It shouldn't be dangling too loosely and open, but it also shouldn't be pulled closed too tightly. This not only helps you breathe better but also relaxes your face, which in turn improves your ability to concentrate throughout the practise.

The seventh point of posture is to let your gaze rest.

After that, you will need to look around two to four feet ahead of you on the floor while maintaining a calm and gentle stare. Try not to concentrate on a single spot or look too intently at the artwork on the wall or the carpet on the floor; instead, simply keep your gaze in a way that is somewhat hazy and relax your eyes. You have the option of closing your eyes in order to eliminate any potential distractions, including the light in the room as well as anything else that may be there.

Before you begin meditating, make a deliberate decision about whether you want to shut your eyes or keep them open. This will help you resist the temptation to fidget and open or close your eyes while you are trying to relax and focus on your breathing. You will only disturb your attention and distract yourself from the task at hand by fidgeting, so either keep your eyes open or shut them, and once you make your decision, be consistent with it. Having said that, if you discover that it is difficult to keep your eyes open during the whole practise, you are free to shut your eyes whenever you feel the need to do so without being too harsh on yourself.

After that, you should get into the habit of meditating. You have a variety of options available to you in terms of contemplative practises; but, if you are just starting out, it is recommended that you focus on ones that are straightforward and uncomplicated. The next will provide you with some simple meditation practises that you are free to engage in whenever you want, whenever you like, and as often you like.

The Site Of Great Prospect

Naomi had finally made it back to the country that God had promised to his people. As the beginning of the barley harvest approached, the area was filled to the brim with the blessings of God. Naomi, however, was under the impression that the LORD had brought her back with nothing. She was under the impression that she was all by herself. She was filled with resentment because of her loss as well as the disappointment she felt over her life. The fact of the matter was, however, that Ruth, her loyal daughter-in-law, was standing by her side the whole time. Ruth had left behind her homeland, her family, and her religious practise in order to pursue an unknown future in a distant continent.

The book of Ruth mentions, for some inexplicable reason, that the Moabite woman Ruth travelled back from the land of Moab. Naomi was not an Israelite, and neither was Ruth. She was a first-time resident of the city of Bethlehem. She had never been to this part of the world before. Ruth had never even stepped foot in the country that God had promised to her, so how could it be said that she had returned to it when she had never been there before? This shows that despite the fact that she was a gentile, Ruth was included in the religious group that was bound by the covenant. We see Ruth's faith shown in the covenant confession found in Ruth 1:16-17. She turned away from her immoral, pagan ways and pledged her allegiance to the God of Israel and the people he had chosen. In the same way that Abraham, who had worshipped the gods of Mesopotamia in the past, was brought by the LORD to the land that was promised to him (Joshua 24:2-3), Ruth also travelled to the country that was promised to her. She follows Abraham's example and seeks a spot to rest on the other side of the Jordan River, in the land of promise given by Yahweh. This land of promise is where she belongs because of her faith, and anywhere one belongs is where one may call "home," thus this place of promise is her home. She is an Israelite by faith, and as such, she is entitled to the land that was given to them by God. As a result, Ruth went back to her hometown, which was a location she had never visited before.

Since individuals who have faith are considered to be offspring of Abraham (Galatians 3:7), Ruth the Moabitess is a daughter of Abraham, who is known as the "father of faith." Because of God's kindness, an outsider who came from Moab, who were Israel's and God's sworn enemies, was adopted into this man's household. This self-sufficient widow, who most likely spoke with a heavy Moabite dialect, asserted that the living God of Israel was her very own by virtue of her faith. This made a huge difference in the outcome. This is the grace of the gospel that God extends to sinners who are looking for a place to call home. When we put our confidence in Christ, Jesus says that he would personally prepare a place for us to rest eternally in his presence (John 14:1-3). This place will be ready when we put our faith in Christ.

CONCEPT OF THE THREE BODIES Presented in Five

This idea is really crucial to comprehending what spirituality is all about. There is just one kind of body that we are aware of working inside of us. This refers to the physical body. The mental body is far more subtle than the physical body. This refers to your astral body. The mental qualities that are a part of us are represented by our astral bodies. The causal body is the third component of our overall body. The causal body is the same as the body of ideas. They make up the whole of the corpus of ideas.

Once we have a firm grasp on the idea of bodies, we will then be able to comprehend the passing of a person. The physical body serves the purpose of the physical life.

After death, the astral body and the causal body become distinct from the physical body. Following physical death, the astral body travels to the astral realm. According to their mental attributes, the majority of humans live in the lower astral plane. We are able to go to the higher astral realm known as hiranyaloka if, after engaging in rigorous Kriya Yoga practises, we are able to achieve nirbikalpasamadhi. Astral hemisphere is surpassed in both elevation and quality by the realm of Hiranyaloka. Hiranyaloka is accessible only to spiritually advanced souls, and only after doing extensive spiritual practises there may the astral body evolve to the point where it can go to the causal realm. The causal world is a far more desirable place to reside than the astral realm.

Now, what is the most important question in life?

What happens after a person has passed away?

When a person dies, their astral and causal bodies become distinct from their physical bodies. Therefore, the journey of the astral body begins after physical death.

The majority of those who are unable to enter the state of nirbikalpasamadhi are nevertheless capable of travelling to the lower astral plane if their karmic channel allows it. Karmic energies tend to gravitate towards the astral planes that are lower in vibration. They must undergo a process of spiritual development in order to progress to higher hemispheres of the astral plane.

Where exactly may one find the astral world?

The astral plane is analogous to a big sphere of magnificent life behind which our material reality exists as if it were a collection of little baskets. Therefore, the trip of awareness from the astral to the physical life repeats itself over and over again in order for us to progress into higher realms of existence. Because of this, we need spiritual energy to enlarge our awareness in order to go with the greater trip that we have to take.

So, let me reassure you, my friends: there is life after death. A fantastic and dazzling life, similar to that of a dream. According to our karmic channel, the astral realm is made up of many different pockets. Hiranyaloka is considered to be the best pocket in the astral universe. This is the bright world where things have reached a very high level of sophistication. However, in order to enter hiranyaloka, we will first need to achieve the condition of nirbikalpasamadhi. To enter Hiranyaloka, a person must first leave their body via the power of their own will, with the assistance of profound meditation, and then release their pranicenergy.This is not suicide; rather, it is the spiritual departure from the body in the state of nirbikalpasamadhi achieved via the use of certain spiritual procedures. Yogis have excellent command of their prana or vital life force energy.

Having Attained Silence And Finding Contentment

Because of the hectic lifestyles that most people lead, the background noise that they experience on a daily basis has likely become something that they can tolerate. But were you aware that one's life may still have moments of stillness even when it is filled with chaos? Keep in mind that allowing certain periods of stillness into your life might bring about a sense of calm when you do so. This is something you can put into practise in your regular life.

Turning off the radio or television and simply sitting motionless in quiet for a few minutes is one example. When there is chaos at home, you may select silence on purpose by refraining from contributing to an already heated dispute. You will benefit from this practise in situations in which it is difficult or impossible to avoid noise.

Therefore, you should step away from the cacophony and pay closer attention to the myriad noises that are occurring around you. When you begin to meditate, you will gradually develop a greater appreciation for what it is like to experience life to the fullest, free from the pressures and ambiguity that often accompany such an endeavour.

At Long Last Discovering Peace

Relax your body and mind completely by settling into a comfortable position. Focus your attention on your breath as you enter your own personal meditative state. When distractions appear, you should just let them flow through your thoughts and then return your focus to where it was before. Stay seated with a calm state of mind and concentrate on observing your breath. Make the most of the natural space you have, and focus on being present in the now. When you make this a consistent part of your life, you will come to understand that you can find inner calm even in the most hectic and harried environments. Keep in mind that the more you do this, the more the quality of your life will improve as a result of your efforts.

Strategies For Meditating For Those Who Are More Experienced

It is common practise to instruct beginners to concentrate and become aware for a relatively little amount of time, anywhere from five to ten minutes. Mindfulness and other forms of mental self-regulation are presented to newcomers. Intermediate practitioners, on the other hand, are able to engage in longer sessions of concentration, mantra, and creative meditation, for example twenty to thirty minutes. Although it can seem simple, maintaining your concentration on a single idea, word, or area of your life for twenty to thirty minutes at a time can be rather tough. Because of this, it is recommended that only practitioners who are already at the intermediate level keep practising for an extended length of time. The following is a list of meditation tactics and practises that are appropriate for practitioners with intermediate levels of experience:

The Practise of Mindfulness Will Help You Become More Aware of Your Feelings – Paying attention to all of the feelings that you are experiencing in the present moment is yet another method of mindfulness meditation that you may put into practise. This is a method of mindfulness that is intermediate in difficulty. In order to put this into practise, you will first need to locate a quiet space in which you can meditate. Take a seat, either on a chair or a cushion. Spend some time bringing your attention to your internal state of mind. Feelings may be described as "joy," "sadness," "anger," or "disappointment," for example. Always keep in mind to categorise it without passing judgement.

Do not criticise yourself for experiencing negative emotions such as sadness, anger, or disappointment. It's sufficient to just recognise all of those sensations before moving on. Spend around five minutes every day engaging in this activity. If you tend to let your emotions get the best of you, you should try this strategy. Your sentiments and emotions will be easier to manage with the aid of this strategy. It will assist you in developing a greater sense of detachment from your sensations and emotions. Daily practise of this might last anywhere from fifteen to twenty minutes.

method for Cravings Control Meditation — This method is for intermediate practitioners who have gained adequate self-awareness and control over their thoughts. Cravings control meditation is for those who have developed sufficient self-discipline. This method is often used in addiction support groups and treatment facilities, such as Alcoholics Anonymous and other similar organisations. To do this, you will need to choose a chair that is comfortable for you and concentrate on being aware of your impulses. Do you have the impulse to eat excessively all at once? Do you find yourself hankering for a glass or two of anything alcoholic? Do you feel the desire to consume drugs that might hurt you or that are illegal? Label the cravings as you become more aware of them, and then let them pass without passing judgement on them. Instead of giving in to the temptation or want, focus on the hope that it would go away. At the first sign of a destructive impulse, gently redirect your attention to an affirmation that the urge will eventually pass. People who are fighting an addiction to alcohol or drugs may make use of this incredibly effective method to help them break free of their dependency. People who desire to enhance their sensitivity to distractions while simultaneously strengthening their willpower might benefit from using this strategy. Daily practise of this might last anywhere from fifteen to twenty minutes.

After completing the asanas, or the physical component of yoga, practitioners of yoga will typically engage in a meditation method known as guided imagery. Guided visualisation is another name for this meditation technique. In the practise of guided imagery, you are often practising under the supervision of a meditation or yoga instructor. This person will direct you to envision soothing images such as a white light, a beach, or a forest while you are doing your meditation or yoga practise.

The widely held belief in psychology that there is a strong connection between the mind and the body serves as the foundation for guided imagery. It is predicated on the idea that everything you can conceive of in your mind may be experienced by your body as if it were real. Imagine every aspect of an orange, including its hue, consistency, peel, and aroma. This is an example of one of the most fundamental types of visualisation methods, which psychologists and medical specialists employ to explain this concept. After then, the physicians will ask you to imagine what it would be like to smell and taste an orange. If you do this, you will notice that you will experience the same tingling sensation as you would get while eating a real orange. This is because the two sensations are identical. This provides irrefutable proof that your body perceives something that is just in your mind as being real. The primary purposes of guided imagery are to reduce feelings of tension and to relax the body. This kind of meditation is also employed by a significant number of people who practise the law of attraction.

Meditation with Mantras - There are a lot of different ways to meditate with mantras. One of the most well-known forms of meditation is called Transcendental Meditation, and it is used by a large number of famous people and successful businesspeople. To put this strategy into practise, locate a supportive chair or a cushion and sit there. You could try closing your eyes and taking several deep breaths. First, bring your attention to your breathing, and after you've done that, start reciting a mantra in your head. You may say the word "love" or "peace" over and over again. The Sanskrit phrases "Baba Nam Kevalam" and "Love is all there is" are often chanted by meditators who have reached an intermediate level of practise. When engaging in this method, you are required to concentrate wholly on the mantra. Bring your attention back to your mantra if you find that your mind is wandering or you find that you are thinking about meaningless things. When you are ready to wrap up the meeting, take a moment to offer a brief prayer of thanks. This kind of meditation is appropriate for intermediate practitioners and may be practised for a total of 40 minutes, twice daily.

Studies have shown that these procedures do not have any affects on a person's mental state, physical state, or psychological state at all. These techniques are safe to use in general. It doesn't matter where you do it—at home, at a yoga studio, on the beach, or in your garden—you'll get the same benefits.

Acquiring Knowledge Of The Chakra System

The name "chakra" derives from the Sanskrit word for "wheel," and it is often shown as a rotating energy hub. Chakras are in a state of constant mobility, continuously taking in and releasing energy. The energy that is sucked in by the chakras originates from the cosmos itself and may be found everywhere, transcending the concepts of space and time that are associated with the physical world. Each energy wheel is responsible for driving a unique set of functions inside the body and personality, including the intellect and the spirit. From the base chakra (which represents Mother Earth) all the way up to the crown chakra, energy should be moving upward via the spine.

When one of the seven chakras in the body gets blocked or is out of harmony with the others, this may lead to a variety of issues. These may take on several forms; for example, if one of your chakras is blocked, it may have an effect on your physical health, your emotional well-being, the states your mind is in, or your spirituality. Or it might have an effect on all of them at the same time. As we are going to see, being aware of the symptoms that you are going through might be a hint of which chakras you need to focus on in order to cure yourself via practises like meditation, yoga, and the use of crystals. Affirmations are another tool that may assist you in regaining the health of your chakras and bringing them back into harmony.

There are many different things that have the potential to obstruct the chakras. Adversity or abuse experienced throughout childhood, for instance, may leave long-lasting marks on the chakras. Recent occurrences have the potential to block chakras as well. The good news is that regardless of what caused the chakras to become blocked, there are tried-and-true methods that may encourage healing and unblock chakras.

Eastern philosophies, in contrast to western medicine, focus on the well-being of the full person and acknowledge that we are not only physical beings but also spiritual and energetic beings. Of course, this does not imply that there is no role for conventional western medicine in the world. Due to the fact that chakra healing and western medicine operate in fundamentally distinct ways, combining the two may be done with relative ease. The healing of one's chakras may be all that is required in many situations, particularly those in which mental and emotional disorders are involved.

In this book, we will go through each of the chakras in great depth and cover the whole book. However, in this section, we will present a brief overview of the characteristics that are linked with each chakra. This will assist you in establishing a connection between the symptoms and imbalances that you are experiencing in your life and each of the seven chakras.

Put Yourself in the Position of Another Person

You will become a better listener and polish your intuitive talents when you are able to remove yourself from the issue and get some distance from it. This compels you to put yourself in their shoes and consider how you would respond to the challenges they face while keeping in mind how you would handle similar events in your own life.

Participating in this activity may increase one's knowledge of others on several levels. While you are listening to other people's accounts of their experiences, you will gain the ability to see the same events and circumstances through a broader lens. Another advantage is that you will likely be less judgemental after gaining a better understanding of this individual, which in turn will allow you to get a deeper knowledge of other people.

You will come to understand at the end of the day that every individual who walks this globe has issues of some kind. Nobody is free from this reality, and there are often issues that persist for a considerable amount of time, whether they are caused by the complexity of the situation or the fact that they are being ignored. This may also help you feel more appreciative for the challenges that you have, and it's possible that they are not as difficult as you had originally imagined they were going to be.

Putting yourself in the position of another person has the additional benefit of making you more patient. Sometimes discussing about difficulties may be difficult, especially if they are intricate or difficult to put into words. This may be because the issues themselves are complex. You will develop more patience as you attempt to comprehend what the other person is going through while you wait for them to get up the nerve and figure out how to tell their tale.

Find people who share your values.
Many times, persons who are psychic may have feelings of isolation from their family members or from other people who they interact with on a regular basis. On the other hand, it is quite probable that you will have another family member that has the same skills as you have. When you inquire about the strategies that they do to hone their own intuitive abilities, they will prove to be an invaluable mentor. As a result of the high likelihood that they have been through the same or a scenario quite similar to what you are going through, they are in a unique position to assist you with the problems that you are having.

Additionally, those who are more in tune with their intuitive selves are able to pick up on the vibrations of one another. It is probable that many of them will be pulled to you in the same way that you will be drawn to many of them. Not only will you feel more safe in your intuitive abilities as a result of building a network of individuals with whom you can connect, but this will also provide you with a support system, which is something that is very important. You will be able to assist each other stay on the straight and narrow because they will tell you if you appear off or offer you strategies to develop your abilities that have worked for them in the past. This will allow you to help each other stay on the straight and narrow.

Examine both your thinking and your beliefs.

Take a good, hard look at the foundation on which your ideas and thoughts are based, since these are the things that will ultimately form the environment both within and outside of you. This covers everything that requires evident attention, such as recurrent cycles of unlearned lessons, as well as elements of oneself that are more concealed from view. Now is the moment to be truthful with yourself, so do that. You won't be able to improve your connection not just with yourself but also with the people around you until you reach this point.

The manner in which you interact with other people is directly impacted when you have preconceived notions and opinions that are not supported by any evidence. When you have dealt with these problems head-on, you will be in a better position to provide assistance to others in a manner that is more connected. Additionally, it will help you become more objective regarding the circumstances you find yourself in.

If you are having trouble locating things that need attention, make it a point to dive further into the matter. We all have preconceived notions about others, whether they be based on age, colour, or gender. Every single one of us is a one-of-a-kind being with our own set of distinctive qualities that we offer to the table. If you make the most of this chance to learn and develop, you will find that your empathy is enhanced even more.

Make the most of this chance to free yourself from the detrimental ideas, attitudes, and beliefs that are no longer in your best interest. Your attitude and your level of development will be hampered by any kind of negativity. When you allow yourself to entertain these unfavourable ideas, you are impacting your surroundings all the way down to the neurochemical level. This has repercussions for your organs, your body as a whole, and your mental attitude, and it also spills out into the world around you.

A Short Meditation Session Of Five Minutes Each Time There Is A Break In The Workplace

Step One: Make use of the chair that you spend the most of your time in while at work. It is true that in order to meditate, you do not even have to go away from the location where you will be completing the most of your job.

In the second step, count each breath that you take. You are going to want to close your eyes and begin the process of counting your breaths while remaining quiet. It is important to keep in mind that one round consists of one inhale and one exhale. It is imperative that you remember to keep counting after each and every breath.

Step Three: Pay attention to how you breathe. You need to use a clock app or set a timer to the meditation period that you wish, in this example five minutes, so that you do not get distracted throughout the course of your meditation by worrying about how much time has gone. Counting those breaths is all that is required of you, just like we went over in the previous point in this discussion.

Let's have a look at a different kind of meditation that we may practise effectively during our five minutes of downtime throughout the day.

A brief five-minute meditation to be done in the workplace around lunchtime.

The first thing you should do is shut your eyes slowly while your phone is set to alarm for a duration of five minutes.

Step Two: When you are seated in that chair of yours, check to see that both of your feet are flat on the ground and that your back is straight. Make sure that the palms of your hands are facing upwards while they are resting gently on your knees.

Step Three: Close your eyes and take three slow, deep breaths, inhaling through your nose and all the way into the bottom of your lungs. Do this for the duration of step three. You should hold your breath for the count of three, and then let it out through your lips on the count of three, continuing to exhale for another three counts after that.

Step Four: Ensure that you keep up with this exercise by breathing for three counts, holding for three counts, and expelling for three counts, all while holding your out breath for three seconds at a time.

Step Five: When the alarm goes off, take three long breathes in through your nose and then exhale through your mouth. Repeat this process three times. The next step is to slowly open your eyes.

There will be occasions when you will need to deliver a significant presentation, and it would be to your great advantage if you could engage in a nice five minute meditation that would help you centre your mind and enable you to make that presentation to the best of your ability. There will be moments when you will have to give an important presentation. This entails meditating to music, which will help to relax your mind in a manner that nothing else can, while at the same time leaving you thrilled to the point where you will be able to give that all-important presentation. Let's investigate the several ways in which we may be sure of this.

What Is It And Why Should I Do It?

The more you know, the more power you have. I have always been of the opinion that it is beneficial to have a solid grasp of precisely how something operates. The purpose of this is to provide you with a deeper knowledge of meditation as well as the many advantages associated with it. You will first get an understanding of the fundamental tenets of meditation before beginning the actual practise of meditation.

Meditation is like exercise for the mind; it helps it build the capabilities and capacities it needs to be able to find solutions to the challenges it faces. In the same way that there are many different treatments available for the many different ailments that may affect the body, there are many different forms of meditation available for the many different issues that can affect the mind.

I am not aware of the specific motivation that brings you to this location today to read this book. Nevertheless, I am aware that it is related to the stressors that come with coping with this existence. I don't know whether you simply want to get rid of your stress or if you are seeking for a means to boost your performance, but I do know that meditation can assist with whatever it is that you are trying to do.

The method of meditation that is presented in this book is a skill that is aimed at fixing the most fundamental issue that the mind faces, which is the stress and suffering that the mind causes on itself by the ideas and acts that it has. Even if we all want for peace and quiet, we nevertheless manage to cause a lot of anxiety and pain for ourselves. This is despite the fact that we all have this wish. Everything arises from the fact that we were brought up to believe that we need to put in a lot of effort in order to be happy. In order for us to achieve our goals and become successful in this world, we have to ensure that we are at the very top. We let ourselves get consumed by all of these concerns to the point that we either forget to look for ourselves or become too busy to do so. The burden of the world begins to press down on us. This serves as a helpful reminder that escaping from that predicament is not impossible. When you meditate, you become more aware of all the factors that contribute to your state of unhappiness and exhaustion. After that, it assists you in curing them.

Seven: Exercises in Meditative Practise

Please be aware that some of these contemplations are rather long. Before you even start to do the exercises, you need first have a good understanding of what they include. It is advised that you read through these meditations out loud while recording them on a voice recorder so that you do not have to attempt to remember each step while you are meditating. This will allow you to focus entirely on the experience of meditation rather than on trying to remember the steps.

We are going to begin with a fundamental meditation known as the breath meditation. It is strongly suggested that you become proficient in this meditation technique before trying any of the others. You will get the abilities necessary to effectively complete the following meditations once you have completed this meditation. When you have reached a point in the breath meditation where you feel at ease, you may go on to the others.

Additionally, the meditations that follow are sorted according to difficulty, with the most challenging meditations being the final two.

Meditation with Complete Concentration
Meditation on the breath
1. Locate a spot that is both peaceful and comfortable to sit in. You want to ensure that you are sitting erect while yet being able to relax completely.
2. Place your palms down on the floor in front of your thighs and rest your hands there. Make sure that you are gazing down about six feet in front of you when you make this adjustment. Keep a calm and easy look, and make an effort not to tense up or put in extra effort at any point throughout this exercise.
3. While maintaining a regular breathing pattern, bring your attention to your breath by concentrating on the feelings that arise during inhalation and

exhalation. Keep your awareness focused on the object of your sight.

4. Give yourself permission to relax in the pause that follows your exhalation and before your next inhalation.

5. While you are concentrating on your breath, pay attention to any thoughts or sensations that come to your attention in that time. In the event that a thought enters your mind, just repeat "thinking" to yourself in your head and then direct your focus back to your breathing. There are some persons who would rather not speak at all and keep to themselves. They just bring their focus back to the breath at that point instead. It does not matter whatever approach you use; what matters is that you do what seems natural to you.

6. If you notice that you are regularly sidetracked by ideas, do not give up or feel disheartened by this fact. Your capacity to focus will improve with each

incident in which you allow yourself to get preoccupied with an idea but then force yourself to bring your attention back to your breathing. This physical activity may be performed with the eyes closed, which may make it simpler for certain individuals to carry out. If you want to enhance your capacity to focus more quickly, you may do this exercise with your eyes open after you have practised it with your eyes closed first.

7. Increase the time of your meditation as your ability to focus on your breath increases.

Meditation with the purpose of concentrating on something

1. Get started with the breath meditation and do it regularly.
2. When you are ready to begin this meditation, you should open your eyes if you have been performing the breath meditation with them closed.

3. Choose an item from your surroundings that you would like to use as the focus of your meditation (Note: You may find it helpful to position an object in front of you before beginning the breath meditation). The item that you decide to use may be whatever you want it to be, such as a candle, a personal keepsake, a picture, a flower, or something else entirely.

4. While looking at the thing, keep your attention on the breath that you are taking. Maintain a calm demeanour and a kind glance while you are staring at the thing. Instead of fixing your eyes directly on the thing, try letting the object draw your attention to itself.

5. Refrain from affixing any label to the thing you are watching while you are doing so. Do not attempt to recognise it, describe it, examine it, or evaluate it in any way. Take this guideline to heart in terms of how you interact with yourself.

Avoid passing judgement on either yourself or this activity. Don't worry about whether or not you're meeting your expectations, and don't second-guess yourself. Just let yourself be completely present with the thing you're looking at. Let all that can be experienced go place without stopping it.

6. If you realise that you are becoming distracted, direct your focus back to the subject you were looking at or to your breathing. If you find yourself focusing on your breathing instead of the item, just shift your attention back. Perform this action as often as is required.

Techniques For Beginners Of Meditation

It is recommended that you begin your meditation practise with mindfulness meditation if you are just getting started. Meditation on present experiences, often known as mindfulness meditation, is one of the most popular and accessible types of meditation.

Remember the steps that we covered in the previous s so that you may get started with your meditation. When you meditate, you should make sure that you are neither too full nor undernourished. In addition to this, check that you are well hydrated and that you are dressed in loose, comfortable clothing.

1. The Most Fundamental Practise of Mindfulness - Take a seat on a chair or a cushion if you want. Take several slow, deep breaths and bring your attention to your breathing. Maintain awareness and focus on your breathing. If your mind starts to wander and you find yourself

thinking about things like your job, the food you consume, the people you are in relationships with, or anything else, bring your attention back to your breathing. Don't pass judgement on yourself. Simply become aware of the idea, release your attachment to it, and redirect your attention to the breath.

2. A Mindfulness Technique to Heighten and Be Aware of the Body Sensations Sitting on a chair and taking deep breaths is one of the techniques to practise mindfulness meditation. This technique may help you become more aware of the sensations that are occurring in your body. Take note of all the feelings you are experiencing right now in this very now. Take note of the prickling sensation that you experience in your toes or the tension that you feel in your fingers. Spend some time focusing on the feelings that are occurring throughout your whole body, from your head to your toes. Take note of everything that can be heard, seen, smelled, and tasted. You may label them,

but you shouldn't pass judgement on them. Perform this activity every day for at least five minutes. Mindfulness may initially present some difficulties for you, but if you master the skills necessary to train your mind, it will become as natural to you as breathing.

3. The Meditation Technique Known as "Heart of the Rose" This technique is a fundamental kind of concentration meditation that was used by Buddhists from centuries past. You may use any flower, however a rose is recommended for this exercise. Take several slow, deep breaths while seated in a chair that's comfortable for you. Take a good look at the rose's centre, often known as its heart. Place the majority of your focus on the flower, and pay close attention to its shape, colour, and texture. If you find that your thoughts are wandering, try to identify what you are thinking and bring your attention back to the flower. You may practise this kind of meditation for a total of five minutes each day for the first week, after which you can extend

your daily meditation session to ten minutes. This method will assist you in taming and mastering control of your thoughts. This method will assist you in being more present in the here and now as well as more attentive of your thoughts and behaviours. You will find that it is much simpler for you to replace negative ideas with positive ones on a day-to-day basis if you use this strategy.

It is recommended that you set an alarm so that you will not be required to check your watch at random intervals. It is also a wonderful experience to meditate beside a mentor or a loved one. It will be much simpler for you to keep your promise to yourself to meditate on a regular basis if you do it this manner.

Meditation With A Guided Session To Clear Away Mental Clutter

I have all I need to handle any circumstance stored inside me. Inhale, then exhale for a total of twenty seconds. I have earned the right to continue living and trying new things.
I have earned the right to achieve all of my hopes and objectives. I have worked hard enough and should be rewarded with the wonderful things the universe has in store for me. Sincerely thank you for looking out for me up till now, but I'm going to have to release you now. Get moving. I'm going to let you go. Inhale, then exhale for a total of twenty seconds. You look down and see that the armour is beginning to fall apart around your body like dust. And last but not least, you dismantle that armour and remove that obstacle. Your mental obstacles will become easier to overcome with the aid

of this guided meditation session. These roadblocks prohibit you from doing anything from mundane daily duties to your wildest aspirations and most important life objectives.

Try to find somewhere quiet and relaxing to spend your time. Relax in a comfortable position, either sitting or lying down. Take a long, slow breath (twenty seconds).

Straighten out your back to allow your breath to come in a more natural way. You should slowly close your eyes and concentrate on being aware of how your breath sounds. Take a few deep breaths, then let yourself relax. Pay close attention to the air that goes into and out of your body for the next twenty seconds.

Take a long, deep breath in and then let it out, focusing on the sensation of the bad energy leaving you along with the air. Take one more breath in, and then gently let out the air. (thirty seconds)

Take a few more slow, deep breaths, and focus on letting go of anything that isn't yours for the next twenty seconds. Keep still, shut your eyes, give in to the unknown, and listen to the voice of your heart as it speaks to you. Take a moment to pause, breathe, and unwind.

Watch as a battleground takes shape in the shadows, and imagine that you are standing smack dab in the centre of it, protected by armour that wraps around your whole body. You are completely impervious to harm when wearing this armour. You are not the recipient of anything. You continue to move stealthily around the battlefield, dodging both humans and arrows, yet you sustain no damage and experience no harm. Inhale, then exhale for a total of twenty seconds. Observe that some of the arrows lead to desirable outcomes, such as the job of your dreams, the relationship of your dreams, and even the amount of money you've always desired.

Take a moment to pause, breathe, and unwind. You'll find that some arrows carry the items you want. What exactly are these items? Expensive things like automobiles, mansions, and vacations to unusual destinations. The other arrows provide chances for you to develop personally, reach your full potential, and become a better person.

These arrows are carrying wonderful and one-of-a-kind experiences, but they will not reach you. And not a single one of them can harm you since your armour shields you from harm, making it impossible for anything useful to strike you.

Then you come to the conclusion that it is not beneficial to continue to hide behind this armour. You have the desire to set yourself free, experience, and prevail.

You have the desire to participate in novel activities. You want to mess up, figure out how to fix it, and go on with your life. Take a moment to breathe deeply (around 20 seconds). And then you say, "I thank you for the protection that I have received up until this point. I thank you for the mental and emotional blocks that have accompanied me up until this point, and I let them go today."

I don't need your assistance any more. From this point on, I will be OK without you.

You are now able to breathe in the unadulterated rural air here in the countryside. You come to the realisation that you are no longer within the armour, and that you are instead outside it. It is the playing field of life, and it is brimming with options, possibilities, and wonderful things that are rightfully yours. You are aware of the wind blowing across your face. You get the impression that you are free.

You are now able to feel the warmth of the sun on your skin as you listen to the sounds of the birds and the wind on the leaves of the trees around you. You come to appreciate how wonderful it is to be alive.

You also make a promise to yourself that if a barrier presents itself in the future, you will immediately recognise it and conduct an investigation into why it is there, where it originated, and what it is attempting to protect you from.

After that, you will express your gratitude to him for the protection and then release him. You won't have any problems as long as you're aware that you don't need it any more. You are going to come back to the here and now when I reach the number five on my countdown, so please stay focused.

Countdown: one, two, three, four, and five. This meditation is available to you anytime you feel the need for it. Take a long, slow, and deep breath (twenty-five seconds).

- A Hands-on Healing Session Inspired by the Raphaelite Work

The Raphaelite Work healing session will begin with a pre-session interview. The purpose of this interview is to orient both the client and the practitioner to a point from which to start the session. The Raphaelite Work practitioner will apply gentle pressure to particular areas on the client's body that correspond to the elements of earth, water, fire, air, and ether while the client is fully clothed and laying on a massage table or a futon on the floor. A discussion of any sensations, ideas, or sentiments that may come up may be facilitated with the help of these points. After the Hands-on Healing session, the client will participate in a post-session interview. During this time, the practitioner will assist the client in integrating the knowledge gained from the five domains, observe how the energy is moving, and identify any shifts that may have taken place within the domains.

- A One-on-One Healing Session Based on the Raphaelite Work

The client and the One-on-One facilitator start a conversation that centres on the client's relationship to the experiences he or she has had with each of the five domains. Clarity will develop for the client in both her or his awareness of self and her or his connection to others as a result of a healing presence being provided in a one-to-one session. The One-to-One facilitator will utilise breath and inquiry to create a peaceful, non-directive, and non-judgmental environment. The facilitator will listen from the heart, using love and compassion, and will enable the client to feel at ease. The facilitator does not provide guidance, express views, or get personally engaged in the process of the client in any way.

- The Retreat for the Work of the Raphaelites

The Raphaelite Retreat provides time and space for participants to be alone with themselves while also facilitating in-depth exploration of the language and flow of energies within each of the five domains. This is accomplished with the assistance of a guide who has completed the Raphaelite Work Retreat. The activities of daily life are left behind at the retreat, and participants are encouraged to direct their focus inward with the help of the staff. The Raphaelite Work Retreat offers participants a better degree of mental acuity with which to cope with the challenges that they face in their day-to-day lives by strengthening and expanding the connection between themselves and their lives. A new sense of self may develop via the use of practises involving breath and presence, and by working within the five domains, which can lead to the emergence of a new sensation of pleasure. A retreat of at least five days is highly suggested; however, retreats of shorter length may also be organised.

Putting Together The Day

This is a really significant point for me. A strategy that allows one to not only get through the day but also to enjoy it. It is using the same concepts of moving away from thinking about the majority of things we prefer to think about - the past, the present, and the future – and instead focusing on the straightforwardness of the current moment. What if, instead of getting up on Monday morning – or, better yet, doing what we are so good at, which is beginning to stress out on Sunday after lunch – we chunked up the day into bits that were more manageable?

Are you becoming anxious about the next week? Then you need to shift your viewpoint. This is your mind's way of telling you that the next week is going to be too much for you to manage at this point in time. Instead, why don't you simply take a little mouthful of it?

You may adjust your viewpoint in this manner, and as a result, become more aware of the here and now by doing so. A strategy for doing things one step at a time rather than attempting to deal with everything all at once.

Bring yourself up to the time of lunch. Maintain your focus on making it through that first encounter. Visit the grocery shop on your hectic Saturday; there is no need to worry about the activities that will take place later in the day. Don't waste your energy at seven in the morning worrying about what's going to happen at dinner; you'll get there eventually, and whatever happens there is going to happen, so there's no use in worrying about it too much in advance.

And getting through it is not the only objective here. We devote a significant portion of our time to thinking about things in this manner: attempting to get through the day as if it were an item to be checked off on a to-do list. However, do we really want to approach each day as if it were a burden?

In an ideal world, we would simply let everything unfold naturally, going from one moment to the next and allowing things to take place in the order in which they are meant to take place.

When you're having one of those days when you find yourself thinking, "I can't wait for this to be over," we should try to keep our attention on the duties at hand rather than constantly going through mental playthroughs of the remainder of the day in your head. We have to overcome the habit of always feeling the need to conduct a mental rehearsal of whatever it is that we are about to do before really doing it. If anything, the likelihood is that being obsessed with anything will actually make us feel more anxious and tense, as well as increase the likelihood that we will behave in an unnatural manner while doing it. This is in contrast to the situation in which we just go through our day with a conscious presence.

The past few times I've had to speak in front of people (at a meeting or in a class), I've pushed myself to break out of my typical practise of spending the whole time leading up to that moment rehearsing in my thoughts what it is that I'm going to say. This is a habit that I've had since I was a child and it's something that I still do today. It never made speaking easier, and I would get so caught up in my own ideas that I would miss everything that everyone else had spoken because I was so focused on mine. When I switched to adopting mindfulness instead, I still felt a bit odd, but when I stopped feeling the need to practise, a burden was lifted off of my shoulders.

Now that you mention it, I'm going to attempt to look at my day in the same manner.

There is no need to have one's mind ready for each and every occurrence and circumstance. Just keep in mind that whatever the next step is that has to take place, it will do so at the appropriate moment, and then the day will go on.

#2: Can you explain what soul movements are?

As was discussed in the prior section, the Family Constellations method serves as the foundation for the meditations that are included in this book. The motions of the soul may be felt in these meditations. To elaborate a little bit more on what they are, they are dynamic movements of the soul that include the transformation and transmutation of the entanglements into an enhanced form of energy. We are all interconnected parts of a vast network that includes not just our own generation but also the generations who came before us in our genetic lineage. These ancestors had full lives and went through their fair share of events, some of which may have been joyful while others may have been tragic. This information is all encoded in our DNA and is handed down to subsequent generations. There is a larger area referred to as "The Knowing Field," and all of this knowledge is also included inside there. One way to put it is to state that the DNA and the knowing field are intertwined with one another.

This comprehensive structure is referred to as the Family structure, and it functions according to the Natural Laws of the Family System. The Family System is comprised of all members, including our parents, grandparents, and ancestors as well as unborn infants, victims, and perpetrators. We are all devoted to our own systems because we feel that they are our home. Belongingness is one of the laws of the Family System that is considered to be one of the most significant laws since it indicates that every single being, regardless of whether they were born or not (in the case of abortions or miscarriages), belongs to the system, and everyone has their own specific role within the system. Nobody can step into another person's shoes, and nobody can assume someone else's position in a group. We are all a part of this community, and we each have a special place within it. For instance, we cannot take the position of our deceased siblings in the lives of our parents, and a mother cannot take the place of a deceased father in the lives of her children. LOVE and LIFE are the two components that have to be able to move freely throughout the system. If their flow is disrupted in any way by any actions that cause an imbalance, then the system will make an effort to naturally restore the equilibrium that was lost. As an example, when there were victims of the Holocaust, their relatives took on the pain that these victims went through since the victims' suffering was disrupting the flow of love. It is understandable that on the surface it may seem as if we are being harsh on ourselves or that we are punishing ourselves. When this happens, the Movements of the Soul may assist in releasing the hidden traumas and suffering that have been stored inside the system.

The things that our ancestors went through were of a profound and diverse kind. Their wounds, limits, and unresolved feelings continue to live on inside us, deep beneath the molecular memories of our bodies. These movements of the soul may assist us in releasing energy entanglements that are not directly connected to us or our own experiences in a way that allows us to go on with our lives.

We might also consider the system to be a Big Soul, in which everyone of us has a certain function to fulfil. However, there are times when in order for us to be made whole and finished, we need to allow the healing energy operate on the fundamental level. This means that the natural laws need to be reinstated, and there should be an unbroken flow of love. These deep wounds and imprints cannot be seen on the surface level, yet they keep recurring in our life as patterns. This is where the Movements of the Soul may be of tremendous assistance since they remove these deep scars and imprints. These restricting patterns need to be released, and the system has to let go of the load of sorrow, grief, hatred, and anger, along with many other emotions that are limiting the progress of the system on both the macro and the micro level. It is true that we are born into the system out of love; hence, it is something that has to be repaired. Emotions that aren't dealt with properly function as a brake on our own development as well as the development of our society as a whole. The Big Soul, the Family System, and all of us as individual souls are working towards the same objective, which is to ensure that the flow of life and love remains unimpeded.

The Importance of the Soul's Various Movements

An imprint may be left in our DNA by traumatic experiences or by any form of disruption that occurs in our life, as was previously described. These impressions have an effect not just on ourselves, but also on our offspring. And throughout our lives, the same patterns keep emerging again and over again. In a same way, the adversity and anguish endured by our ancestors is transmitted down to us. We need to restore the ORIGINAL ORDER OF LOVE in the system so that we can understand where these patterns are originating from and so that we can cure them. And in order to bring LOVE back into our lives, we have to heal the wounds and the impressions left by the past. When we practise a certain exercise or meditation that is described in this book, we are really enabling the system to repair itself and break free from the imprints that have been placed on it. The energy imprints that we are holding from the actual victims are also released, so it is not only us who are affected by this. These motions are powerful expressions of the soul, and they assist in the dissolving of these wounds and entanglements in a manner that is incomprehensible to rational thought. At other times, they are profound emotions that are difficult to intellectualise or express via words. You need to give yourself permission to totally submerge yourself in the experience so that you can get the most out of it.

One illustration that may help to clarify this phenomenon is as follows:
The premature death of one of a child's twins occurred during the seventh month of the mother's pregnancy; yet, the mother was required to continue carrying the deceased kid until the birth of the second child. At the time of the kid's birth, the mother experienced a range of emotions, including joy but also sadness for the loss of her other child. The situation with the father was the

same. During the whole duration of the pregnancy, the parents were terrified about the prospect of caring for two children at the same time, which caused the newly born child to feel as if he or she is carrying a burden since his or her sibling had to give up their life. They were concerned about the status of their finances as well as the added weight of duties that would come with having two children. Both of them were subtly conveying the message that they did not want to have two children but rather just one. The request of the parents for one of the twins to give up his life was granted, and he did so.

In this situation, the other twin is not only processing the emotion of having a heavy destiny, but also the load of the duties, such as shame and sadness, that the parents are projecting onto them in order to deal with it. This surviving youngster is burdened with the feelings of both of his parents, as well as those of his twin brother who passed away. The fact that he now has life as a reward for the other twin's willingness to make the ultimate sacrifice makes him feel as if he is trapped inside an intricate web. In this particular scenario, the infant will be doomed to a difficult destiny and will have a difficult time as an adult. As a result of the fact that the parents have not accepted responsibility for the fact that their other kid sacrificed his life to grant their dream. This has disrupted the natural progression of life and love in the life of the kid who survived.

In the scenario described above, the parents will be able to reestablish the flow of life and love in their relationship with one another and their kid if they accept the responsibility in its entirety, mourn the loss of the child, and do it from the depths of their hearts. It is necessary for both of the kid's parents to make an appropriate atonement for the loss of the child. This phenomenon, which plays a significant role in all of our lives, is referred to as the Movement of the Soul.

www.ingramcontent.com/pod-product-compliance
Lightning Source LLC
Chambersburg PA
CBHW050245120526
44590CB00016B/2229